COLOR FOR
YOUR HOME

By Christine E. Barnes and the Editors of Sunset Books

MENLO PARK • CALIFORNIA

SUNSET BOOKS

Vice President, General Manager: Richard A. Smeby
Vice President, Editorial Director: Bob Doyle
Production Director: Lory Day
Art Director: Vasken Guiragossian

STAFF FOR THIS BOOK

Developmental Editor: Linda J. Selden
Color and Design Consultants: Joan Malter Osburn and
Juliana Edlund
Copy Editor: Marcia Williamson
Design and Page Production: Nina Bookbinder
Principal Photographer: E. Andrew McKinney
Photo Director/Stylist: JoAnn Masaoka Van Atta
Illustrations: Steven Osburn, Osburn Design
Color Rings and Paint Dabs: Christine E. Barnes
Color Palettes: Joan Malter Osburn, Juliana Edlund,
and Christine E. Barnes
Production Coordinator: Patricia S. Williams

10 9 8 7 6 5 4 3 2

First printing September 1999

ISBN 0-376-01264-1
Library of Congress Catalog Card Number: 99-63573
Printed in the United States

For additional copies of *Color for Your Home* or any other Sunset book,
call 1-800-526-5111. Or see our web site at www.sunsetbooks.com

Cover: Blue-violet walls and a blue-violet chaise tell a monochromatic color
story. Although it is considered a cool color, blue-violet is a bit warmer than
true blue. Architect: Alla Kazovsky/Kids, Studio. Cover design by Vasken
Guiragossian. Photograph by E. Andrew McKinney. Photo direction by
JoAnn Masaoka Van Atta.

COLOR HARMONY

Did you know that the human eye can discern more than six million colors? Of course you are not required to know them all—that's a relief!—and in practice you'll use only a handful in your home. Which colors you choose and use—and why—is what this book is about.

As you take in the ideas and concepts on the following pages and begin to formulate your own color plan, push yourself a little. That's right: push yourself. You can always pull back when you get into unfamiliar (and scary) territory. If you venture confidently in the direction of colors that you love, you are sure to meet with more success than if you were timid to begin with. A home that resonates with color harmony will be your reward.

Many individuals and firms had a part in this book. We're particularly grateful to Benjamin Moore Paints, Calico Corners, Heidi Emmett, Tami Miller, Osburn Design, Ruby's Fine Gifts, Sierra Tile & Stone, and Kim Smith of Young's Interiors.

CONTENTS

SPECIAL FEATURES

AT HOME WITH COLOR

Faced with the daunting array of paint chips at your home center, you might decide that white is a good idea after all. White is safe; searching for the just-right color can be confusing.

But the world is a colorful place. Wouldn't it be great to bring some of its vitality into your home, knowing that you'll be pleased with the results? You can. With the help of this book, you can cast aside your fears and begin to see color with fresh eyes. After all, it's the most powerful decorating tool at your disposal. With a little knowledge and a sense of adventure, you can transform your home with color.

Mastering color is easier than you might think. In the pages that follow, you'll find simple concepts and step-by-step strategies for developing your own color plans. You'll quickly discover that there is no such thing as "bad color," just inappropriate color. Appropriateness is as much about the quality of a color—how light or dark, how bright or dull, how warm or cool it is—as the hue itself. You can make almost any colors work when you choose and combine them with these characteristics in mind.

You'll also learn that colors don't exist in isolation. They coexist and interact, and you simply can't predict how they will behave in one another's company until you see them together. That's why it's important to audition potential fabric, flooring, paint, and other samples in your home before buying materials. Think of it as "trying on" color. This fabric works; that paint doesn't. You can almost measure the pleasure as your scheme evolves.

Decorating materials themselves aren't free, but the magic of color is, and any combination is yours for the asking. Be open to the possibilities. With a grasp of the basics and a confident approach, you'll soon feel at home with color—and welcome it into your home.

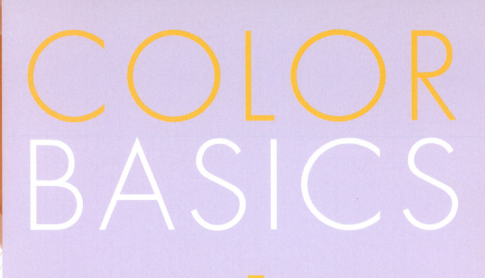

COLOR BASICS

Color wheel? Who needs the color wheel? If that's how you feel about color theory, you have plenty of company. Most of us, when faced with a room in need of a new look, do not think of the science of color. We have two concerns: "Which colors should I use?" and "Where do I put them?" We are afraid—make that terrified—of color.

To develop the skill and confidence to create a room that is quiet but not dull, or vibrant but not garish, you need a good color vocabulary. Although it's difficult—sometimes impossible—to use words to describe what is visual, it's helpful to learn the basic terminology. You also need to get acquainted with the color ring (page 11), a simplified version of the color wheel traditionally used by fine artists. If this already sounds too theoretical, relax. The color concepts we explore here rely on easy-to-understand terms and lots of examples. Take the time to learn the basics; you'll soon understand how to compose rooms you'll love to live in. ■

YOU'LL HAVE MORE SUCCESS CHOOSING AND COMBINING COLORS IF YOU MASTER A FEW TECHNICAL TERMS. THESE REFER TO THE *CHARACTERISTICS* OF COLOR—THE QUALITIES THAT GIVE COLORS PERSONALITY AND CHARACTER.

The Language of COLOR

HUE

Hue is just another word for color. Turquoise and crimson are hues; so are softer colors like lilac and butter cream. The terms hue and color are used interchangeably in art and interior design.

VALUE

Value refers to the lightness or darkness of a color. Of course, there are infinite variations in value, from the lightest lights to the darkest darks. Mint, for example, is a light value of green. Navy is a dark value of blue. If you look at the color ring on page 11, you'll notice that each pure color has a natural value; that is, yellow is naturally light, while violet is naturally dark.

Light-value colors are pale versions of the pure hues. Pink is a light value of red. Peach is a light value of orange. And iris is a light value of blue-violet.

Light-value colors are not limited to colors we call "pastels." Lavender, melon, and coral are light-value colors, but they are stronger than hues you might use in a nursery.

Medium-value colors are midway on the scale of light to dark. If you're having trouble distinguishing medium-value colors, try looking at the colors in question next to lighter and darker versions.

Dark-value colors often have descriptive names—spice, indigo, and walnut, to name a few.

Artists refer to light, medium, and dark values as tints, tones, and shades. Confusion arises because we often use the terms "tone" and "shade" to describe certain colors—"a shade of blue" or "red tones," for example. That's why it's best to think of colors as being light, medium, or dark in value.

RIGHT: Every color has a range of values including lights, mediums, and darks.
BELOW: Painting these recessed windows in dark-value colors makes them seem deeper.

TOP RIGHT: Warm walls and cool-hued cabinetry balance the visual temperature in a contemporary kitchen.
MIDDLE RIGHT: Within each color family, there are warm and cool versions.
BOTTOM RIGHT: Blue, violet, and green are cool; yellow, orange, and red are warm.

TEMPERATURE

This aspect of color is easy to grasp, even for novices. Refer to the color ring on page 11 as you read about visual temperature.

If you draw an imaginary line on the color ring from red-violet to yellow-green, the colors to the left—yellows, reds, and oranges—seem warm. Warm colors are considered to be "advancing" because they seem as though they are coming closer to the viewer. On walls, warm colors can make a room feel cozy and enveloping.

The colors to the right of that imaginary line on the color ring—greens, blues, and violets—are the cool hues. They appear to be farther away, which is why they are called "receding" colors. On walls, cool colors can make a room feel spacious and calm.

Visual temperature is relative. Red-violet and yellow-green may seem warm or cool, depending on the presence of other colors. Next to orange, red-violet looks cool; next to blue, it looks warm.

Visual temperature comes into play when you combine colors in a decorating scheme. In general, the juxtaposition of warm and cool color intensifies each. If you paint one room a warm red and an adjoining room a cool green, each will seem more intensely warm or cool. This effect also works within a room: cool walls make a warm wood floor seem even warmer.

COMPLEMENTARY COMBINATIONS

Complementary combinations are made up of colors that lie directly opposite each other on the color ring. Red and green are complements, as are yellow-orange and blue-violet. The opposing color pairs can be approximately opposite, as well: sage green (a yellow-green) combines beautifully with violet, even though they are not direct complements.

In practice, any color that lies on the opposite side of the color ring will balance and enliven your main color. Blue and orange may look harsh together, but blue works well with yellow, which is on the warm side of the color ring. When you combine complementary colors, feel free to wander around the ring a bit. The effect is still harmonious. In fact, sometimes it's more interesting when the colors are not direct complements.

Schemes made up of complementary primaries and secondaries, such as yellow and violet, seem visually stronger than those consisting of intermediate colors, such as blue-violet and yellow-orange. The presence of two colors in the intermediate hues softens the contrast.

COMPLEX COMBINATIONS

Complex schemes consist of colors spaced around the color ring in a variety of arrangements. Teal, magenta, and mango (intense versions of blue-green, red-violet, and yellow-orange) are equidistant on the color ring, in a combination known as a "triad." A four-color combination of equidistant colors, such as green, red, yellow-orange, and blue-violet, is known as a "tetrad." Complex color schemes are pleasing because they automatically balance visual temperature. To help you imagine these combinations, you might try isolating the colors on one of the color rings while covering the others. For example, using Color Ring #2, cover all of the colors except orange, green, and violet.

Complementary and complex color combinations are trickier than monochromatic or analogous schemes. Use the tips that follow for help.

ABOVE, TOP: Complementary colors—blue and orange are shown here—are best used in unequal quantities. New neutrals expand the scheme.
ABOVE, BOTTOM: A complex combination of green, orange, and violet—colors equidistant on the color ring—is known as a "triad."

COLOR CUE

Complements visually intensify each other. Yellow walls will seem more intense if you paint the trim a pale gray-violet.

COLOR COMBINATION TIPS

All colors go together if you know how to combine them. Sound simple? It is, now that you know about the characteristics of color (pages 8–10). Finding the right colors is as much about choosing harmonious values and intensities as it is specific hues. Just as important are the proportions of colors in a combination. Following are simple guidelines for creating successful schemes. Keep in mind that, although color theory tends to focus on pure colors, in the real world—in your home—colors are almost always softened and diluted.

- *Use similar values to link different colors.* Light colors from all around the color ring naturally go together because they share a common value. That's why willow, maize, and lilac, all light-value colors, are pleasing together. Deep colors, such as claret, spruce, and navy, likewise have an affinity, their dark value. When you use sharply contrasting values in a scheme—dark green furnishings in a white room, for instance—your eye may jump from one element or area to another, an effect you may or may not like.
- *Use similar intensities to link different colors.* In other words, use clear colors with clear colors and grayed colors with grayed colors. Like value, intensity is a unifying factor. Burgundy and hunter, low-intensity versions of red and green, are congenial colors. This approach—combining different colors of similar intensities—is just as effective when the colors are opposite on the color ring as when they are side by side.

Of course, identical values and intensities aren't always desirable—too much sameness can lead to boredom. To a group of light values, throw in

ABOVE: *Vary the intensities and values of bold colors just a bit to soften the contrast.*

LEFT: *A complementary combination of pink (a light value of red) and green is most pleasing when one color is dominant.*

COLOR CUE

When you change color from room to room, choose colors of a similar intensity. The rooms will look different, yet unified.

a few darker colors. Or punch up a low-intensity scheme with a bit of more intense color. Fortunately, with so many materials and textures available, you'll automatically achieve variation in value and intensity when you gather samples.

- *Use your colors in unequal quantities.* Equal amounts of color fight for attention; unequal amounts are more pleasing. A large expanse of green, for example, with smaller amounts of violet and coral, is harmonious, whereas equal quantities of green, violet, and coral are likely to be unpleasantly competitive. The secret is to let one color dominate while the others play supporting roles.

Where you place colors in a room is just as important as their proportions. Imagine pink and green in two hypothetical schemes. One room has pale green walls and soft pink furnishings; the other has pale pink walls and soft green furnishings. Although the same two hues are involved, the effects are dramatically different. For now, as you consider different color combinations, keep in mind that color placement has everything to do with the visual impact of a scheme. In "Step 6: Editing and Auditioning" (pages 58–61), you'll work with the materials you've gathered and make decisions about where to use them in your room.

How Color WORKS

encing other colors and helping to set a mood. Be aware, however, that strongly colored lamp shades tend to soak up the light. White or cream shades have become classic because they yield maximum light.

A room's exposure determines the quality of its natural light, which can influence your color choices. North-facing rooms receive less direct sunlight, and that light tends to be cool, while south-facing rooms get inherently warmer light. The conventional wisdom is to balance the temperature in a room, using warm colors in north-facing rooms and cool colors in south-facing ones. You are free to ignore that advice, of course, and enhance the natural temperature of a room with colors of a similar temperature.

The way materials and surfaces reflect light also affects color. A shiny red lacquer table will reflect light and appear brighter, while the same red rendered in a heavily textured fabric will be comparatively dull.

LEFT: A kitchen bathed in a combination of natural and artificial light has true color rendition.

BELOW: Sconces cast a suffused light, nuancing the violet of the walls. The rafters' downlights help the warm wood tones glow.

COLOR AND LIGHT

Thanks to light, we see color. The science of color and light is not that simple, of course, but a basic understanding of how light influences color can help you make wise color choices.

Most light in your home is artificial, and the color of that light varies. Warm light from incandescent bulbs intensifies yellows and reds but dulls the cooler colors. Halogen bulbs, a special category of incandescents, produce a whiter, brighter light. The cool blue light of standard fluorescent bulbs amplifies blues and greens but muddies warm yellows and reds. Newer "soft white" fluorescents come closer to the warmth of incandescents.

Light fixtures themselves contribute color to a room. Pendant lights can have brightly colored glass. A warm-hued lamp shade will cast its own glow, influ-

Should you paint adjoining rooms the same color or different colors? It all depends on your objective. If you hope to create a smooth visual flow from room to room, consider carrying the same paint color and flooring throughout. If you like the look of layered color and the sense of separation between rooms, use different colors in adjoining rooms. You can combine both approaches by choosing related but different colors for adjoining rooms, such as a light, warm taupe in the living room and a darker, cooler taupe in the dining room.

LEFT: Low-intensity, cool colors make a room seem spacious and serene. Painting the molding and ceiling slightly different gray-blues accentuates the room's architectural features.
BELOW: Using different wall colors of similar values and intensities creates a sense of separate but unified rooms.

COLOR AND SPACE

Using color to define or alter space is really about creating illusions. Once again, the characteristics of color (pages 8–10)—hue, value, temperature, and intensity—come into play. The traditional thinking is that light, cool colors enhance the sense of space, while dark, warm colors make a room seem smaller. Along the same lines, low-intensity colors are thought to make a room seem more spacious, while more intense colors have been thought to contract space.

In real life, many other factors, such as the quantity and quality of the light a room receives, limit these visual effects. Painting the walls a light color will not transform a naturally dark room into an open, airy space. Cool colors will not necessarily expand a tiny room. Sometimes it's best to evaluate what you have—and then go with it rather than against it. If your room is small, why not enhance its coziness with warm color on the walls?

Color can be a useful tool when you want to alter the apparent proportions of a room. Painting an end wall in a long, narrow room a warmer, darker color may create the illusion of a better-proportioned room. In a square room, painting one wall a more intense color and the remaining three walls a less intense color can diminish the boxy look. Again, many variables can conjoin to minimize these effects.

UNDERTONES

Interior designers sometimes say, "This green has blue undertones; that gray is yellowish." Your response is likely to be, "I don't see it." Your next thought might be, "What difference does it make?"

It makes a big difference. The term undertones refers to the subtle, underlying color of a color. How can a color have another color? Few colors, especially those in interiors, are pure. Instead, they are mixtures of several colors, and the undertones reflect that mix. Put another way, the undertone of a mixed color is the minor color that influences the main color. Pure red has no undertones because it is a primary color. But terra-cotta, a version of red-orange, has yellow

undertones. Where does the yellow come from? Red-orange is half orange, and orange is half yellow (see page 11).

Discerning undertones is a challenge for the novice, but practice will sharpen your eye and build your confidence. The key is to really look at colors and analyze their content. Think of it as a game: can you see the red undertones in a blue-violet fabric? (Remember, violet is made up of red and blue.) That hint of red might cue you to consider adding other colors with red undertones, such as peach (made up of red and yellow) or melon (a lighter value of red-orange). Both colors are harmonious with blue-violet.

Undertones are especially important when considering wall color. If you love yellow but are reluctant to use it on your walls, look for a near-white with yellow undertones, a color you might call French vanilla (see "What About White?" on pages 66–67). If you're using a patterned fabric with a neutral background, study its undertones and choose a wall color with a similar color bias.

Neutrals can have undertones, too, and it is often easier to spot the undertones in a neutral than in a more vivid color. Comparing neutrals side by side helps; the green undertones in a greenish gray are obvious next to a true gray, which has no color.

If you're still having trouble identifying the undertones of colors, simplify the exercise and ask yourself, "Are the undertones warm or cool?" That information alone can help you choose compatible hues. Apple green, for instance, has warm undertones; aqua blue has cool undertones.

In reality, identifying undertones is more about avoiding disaster than anything else. Undertones that clash—a bluish white next to a yellowish white, for example—may look unpleasant. Even slight differences in the undertones of wall and trim colors can be noticeable.

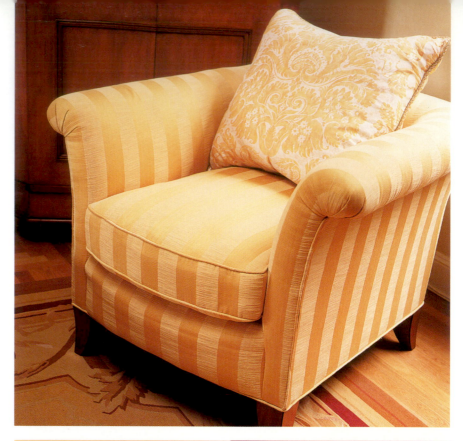

There's nothing like yellow to lift the spirits and lighten the mood. Soft yellows (light-value, low-intensity hues), with names like maize and taffy, are ideally suited to walls and furnishings, where stronger colors might overwhelm. (Wallpaper and fabric with soft yellow backgrounds are perennial favorites.) Pale yellow marries well with soft blues, pinks, and greens, even neutral grays. Bold yellows and formal golds demand equally intense color companions, such as royal blue, crimson red, or primrose pink. When paired with violet, its complement on the color ring (page 11), yellow becomes regal; gentler versions, such as amethyst and butter cream, say "spring."

Yellow-green is a large, extended color family, with many distant relatives. Common names—chartreuse, apple green, and sage— reflect the range of values and intensities you'll find with this versatile hue. Intense yellow-green is a powerful accent—as acid green piping on a pillow, for example, or lime green opaline glass. In the scheme of things (color scheme, that is) light yellow-green teams easily with clear blues and yellows for a summery look. Low-intensity yellow-greens, colors with names like olive drab and willow, harmonize with warm beiges and creamy whites. Red-violet, the color opposite on the color ring (page 11), balances the warmth of yellow-green in a sophisticated complementary relationship.

If nature has a favorite color, it must be green. Many names for green come from plants, among them fir, mint, and fern. Because it is so much a part of the natural world, green looks at home in almost any scheme, especially one that includes warm wood. In the company of yellows, peaches, and pinks, green exerts a cooling influence. Green is just as appropriate with blues and violets, hues on the same side of the color ring (page 11). Although it is a secondary color, made up of equal parts of primary yellow and blue, green is so ubiquitous in decorating that it is sometimes referred to as "the fourth primary" and is often included in palettes of red, yellow, and blue.

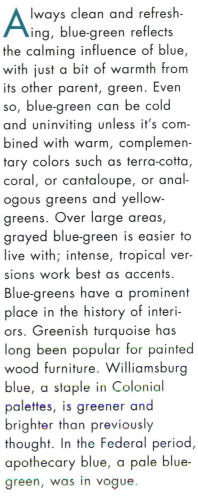

Always clean and refreshing, blue-green reflects the calming influence of blue, with just a bit of warmth from its other parent, green. Even so, blue-green can be cold and uninviting unless it's combined with warm, complementary colors such as terra-cotta, coral, or cantaloupe, or analogous greens and yellow-greens. Over large areas, grayed blue-green is easier to live with; intense, tropical versions work best as accents. Blue-greens have a prominent place in the history of interiors. Greenish turquoise has long been popular for painted wood furniture. Williamsburg blue, a staple in Colonial palettes, is greener and brighter than previously thought. In the Federal period, apothecary blue, a pale blue-green, was in vogue.

The color of summer skies and mountain lakes, blue is always fresh and appealing. Blue is a relatively broad color family, including hues as varied as cornflower, cobalt, and cerulean. Bright, breezy blues please children, while less intense versions satisfy more sophisticated tastes. Blue is the coolest of the cool colors, begging for the company of warmer cohorts: robin's-egg blue is pretty with pink; chambray is balanced by buttercup; navy is enriched by maroon. Analogous blues and greens, once seldom paired, are now popular together in spring and summer palettes. White is a favorite partner for blue, especially in kitchens and bathrooms, where simplicity is desired.

Blue-violet is the color of periwinkle and iris, the lavender-blue of the nursery song. It pairs beautifully with yellow-orange, its complement on the color ring (page 11). (If yellow-orange is difficult to visualize, imagine "cheddar" or "mango.") Intense versions of blue-violet are elegant in combination with gold and creamy white. Although it's considered a cool color, blue-violet is a bit warmer than blue, which may explain its popularity. Teamed with salmon (a light value of red-orange) and apple green (a bright yellow-green), it forms an exquisitely balanced triad (page 17). The use of kindred hues on either side of a color—in this case, violet and red-violet in one direction and blue and blue-green in the other—is always pleasing.

Violet—better known in decorating as purple—has a mixed reputation. Some consider it a magical, mysterious color, while others find it heavy and dreary—particularly the deep, dark violets associated with the Victorian era. Light, romantic hues, such as lilac and lavender, are favored for bedrooms, especially little girls' rooms. Green and yellow (violet's complement on the color ring) are congenial colors, and you often see the three hues together in nature. (Visualize violets in bloom, with yellow centers and green leaves.) Darker versions, such as eggplant and grape, can convey a formal look in combination with cream, gray, and black.

Rarely mentioned as a favorite color, red-violet nevertheless appears often in color schemes, usually as an accent or a subordinate color. Few know it by its color-theory name, but descriptive terms are easy to picture: merlot is a dark value of red-violet, orchid is a light value, and fuchsia is an intense version. Residing between red and violet on the color ring (page 11), red-violet is warmer than violet but cooler than red (thanks to the influence of violet, which is half blue). Complementary yellow-green and red-violet work well together as low-intensity sage and plum. Magenta, black, and white were common decorative companions in Art Deco interiors, while saturated fuchsia, teal, and mango are colors of the tropics.

COLOR ENCYCLOPEDIA: **RED**

Bright and brazen, pure red is the hottest, most visually demanding color on the color ring. A red room pulsates with energy, and all eyes are drawn to red furnishings, accents, and accessories. Pink, a light value of red, is so popular that it almost seems to merit its own place on the color ring. Intense reds benefit from liberal doses of the true neutrals—black, white, and gray; deeper, darker reds, such as cranberry and pomegranate, are quieter in comparison. Rarely used in analogous schemes—red's neighbors are almost as aggressive—red is more likely to be paired with cool green in romantic cottage florals, or used in combination with the other two primaries, yellow and blue.

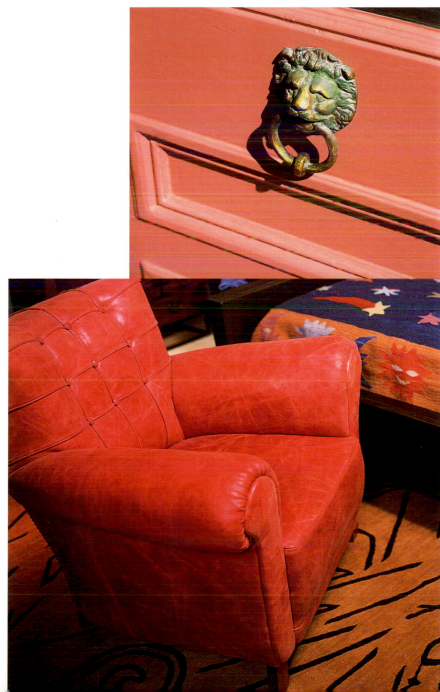

More complex than either of its parent colors, red-orange is warm and welcoming, the color of raw earth and clay pots. Terra-cotta is perhaps the best-known version of red-orange, but it also comes in hues like coral, salmon, and persimmon. In darker values, red-orange turns to russet, burnt umber, and sienna. A natural in rooms where people gather, red-orange can work well on walls, enveloping a room and flattering guests with its glow. Such a warm color begs for cooler hues. A triad (page 17) of terra-cotta, deep periwinkle, and olive satisfies the desire for balance in visual temperature. Used in combination with its complement, blue-green, red-orange is often considered a "Southwest" color.

Full-strength orange is a brash, bold color that conjures up images of fast food and advertising. Few dare to use it "as is" in large quantities, but orange is the source of many more workable hues, such as tangerine, pumpkin, and copper. Lowering the intensity makes orange more livable; in fact, most browns are dark-value, low-intensity versions of orange or red-orange. Complementary orange and blue are often harsh, even when the hues are low-key, but the addition of other colors softens the contrast: imagine pale peach, mint, and lilac or deep cinnamon, juniper, and violet. If too much orange can be overpowering, small amounts can make lively accents—as pillows, candles, or art.

Richer than yellow but less assertive than orange, yellow-orange is perhaps the least-known color on the color ring, yet its luminous, uplifting qualities make it an ideal color for the home. Yellow-orange abounds in nature—imagine the colors of honey, tumeric, and butternut squash. Blond wood, natural wicker, even brass are examples of yellow-orange materials that appear in the home. Yellow-orange lends itself to monochromatic color schemes (page 16) but combines beautifully with blue-green and red-violet, colors equidistant on the color ring (page 11). Imagine them as saturated saffron (yellow-orange), jade (blue-green), and plum (red-violet), or papaya, aqua, and orchid.

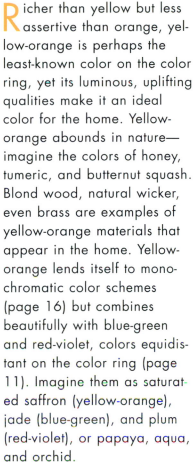

COLOR
STRATEGIES

■

Planning and implementing a color scheme for your home, even for one room, is a significant project, but it need not be intimidating if you break down the process into manageable steps. Notice the word *process*. Choosing a color scheme is not like baking a cake or building a bookshelf from start to finish. Instead, it's a creative experience that evolves according to the givens in your home (those furnishings or artworks or architectural features you plan to keep or must work with), your decorating goals, and your color preferences. There are no hard-and-fast rules or must-do sequence for this process, and you are free to follow the steps advised here in the order that makes the most sense in your situation. But there are approaches—call them strategies, if you will—that make the color-selecting experience easier and more fun. Begin at the beginning, with your wish list. ■

STEP 1:

At the very start of your project, your first question is likely to be, "What am I going to do?" This question usually goes hand-in-hand with, "How much can I afford to do?" Start by drawing up a wish list. At the top of your list will be your givens. Does the sofa stay? Do you have an heirloom rug? Beautiful flooring? Noteworthy window frames? Although they may appear to be drawbacks, givens are actually a gift because they provide a place to begin. All decisions that follow depend in part on your givens.

Having decided what to keep, focus on what you hope to achieve. Think big at this stage; dreaming is free, and you can always scale back as you get into a project. Will you redo just the living room and dining room? The entire house? Are you keeping the carpet (a given) but changing the wall color (a variable)? As you make decisions, your wish list will change. A beautiful fabric for a chair may lead to new window treatments. The prospect of new flooring in one room may tempt you to carry it into adjoining rooms. Decorating is contagious, and your wish list is bound to grow. A typical list might include:

- furniture, including hard furnishings, such as tables, and upholstered pieces
- wall color, either plain paint or a decorative finish
- wall coverings, such as wallpaper and fabric
- flooring, such as carpet, wood, vinyl, or tile
- window treatments, including hard treatments, such as blinds, shades, or shutters, and soft treatments made of fabric
- countertops and cabinets
- accents, accessories, and art
- lighting design and fixtures

If you're on a limited budget, list those things that will make the most difference, such as new wall color and a new sofa, then add to the scheme as your resources permit. It's fun, but not necessary, to do it all at once. Taking your time can prevent costly and discouraging mistakes.

As much as possible, let go of those things you don't like but feel you should keep because they are "still good" or were expensive. It's usually a mistake to make do with something just to save money. If you have favorite pieces that won't work in your new scheme, use them in another room or put them away for a while. If a chair is dated and no longer fits in with your plans, get rid of it. You can sometimes alter a given to adapt it to your new scheme.

Making a Wish List

TOP LEFT: *An intricate tile floor offers a way to use color, pattern, and texture where they're least expected.*

FAR LEFT: *Although accessories are usually small, they can play a major role in a room. The boldly scaled floral pillow adds pattern and texture to a subdued ticking-covered sofa.*

ABOVE: *When you make up your wish list, think "theme and variation." Crackle-glazed paint, gauzy window treatments, golden-toned woods, and a new–neutral chair are different enough to be interesting, yet similar enough to look unified.*

NEAR LEFT: *Wall color need not be solid. A pigmented shellac paint finish creates a rich textural look.*

We take for granted the space we live in—until we're ready to change it. Then all sorts of questions pop up. To best assess your room or rooms, ask yourself the following:

- Where are your opportunities to use color? The walls and floor are the most obvious, and changes in these surfaces will have the greatest visual impact. Furnishings, both soft and hard, are other places to make a statement with color. Even something as small as a window sill can contribute color. If you take the time to look, you'll see that color is everywhere—in a fabric, a light fixture, or a wood floor.

- What are the architectural features of the room? Do you have a fireplace that commands attention? Is the molding interesting? Are there handsome hardwood floors? The walls, ceiling, trim, and floor are the bare bones of a room and the foundation of any decorating scheme. If your room has interesting architectural features, you'll want to play them up. If not, consider minimizing them by painting them the same color as the walls.

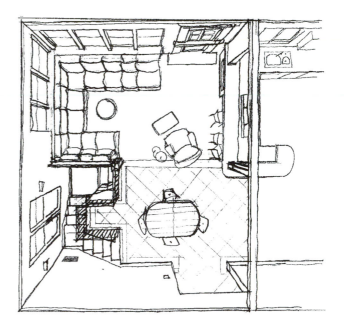

STEP 2:

LEFT: A tiled fireplace inspired color ideas for bar stools, soft furnishings, and display pieces.

BOTTOM LEFT: An open living space presents design challenges, and color can help unify the scheme.

BOTTOM MIDDLE: A sketch of your room can help you assess your space; later, it can help you determine where to place color.

BELOW: A vaulted great room calls for an assertive use of color and lighting. Red trim dramatically defines the space; the lighting design brightens light-value walls while highlighting the panel of art.

- Is your room bathed in natural light, or do you rely on artificial light? Light affects our impression of color and helps set the mood in a room. (See "Color and Light," page 20.) Be sure to notice how the light changes during the day, from morning to night.

- How do you and your family use the space? A room that's used by the entire family calls for colors that will meet with everyone's approval. In individual rooms, let family members choose their own color schemes.

- If your decorating plans include several rooms, how do they relate to one another? An entry, for instance, usually leads to a living room, which often adjoins a dining room. A family room may connect to the kitchen. Stand in the doorways of connecting rooms and study the visual flow. Strive for smooth transitions, even if you plan to paint adjoining rooms different colors. Rooms that relate, even in a subtle way, create a sense of unity.

A bird's-eye-view sketch of your room or rooms, including measurements, can help you see the space you have to work with. A sketch done to scale on graph paper is ideal, but you can also draw something as simple as a rectangle to represent a room, with connecting rectangles to represent adjoining rooms. Add furnishings, both existing and planned-for, to your sketch to better understand their relationship to the room and other furnishings.

After you've done your sketch, consider a radical step. Take all the furnishings out of the room and look at it empty. When you remove familiar furnishings, you'll see possibilities that don't emerge when the room is full.

Assessing Your Space

ABOVE: Cool, low-intensity color is restful in a bedroom suite. Using different values from one space to another creates a sense of depth.

ABOVE RIGHT: Intense yellow is a vibrant choice for a country kitchen bathed in natural light.

RIGHT: A cool, low-intensity dining room with grayed green walls sets a quiet, traditional mood. The same space would look—and feel—entirely different dressed in warm, pure colors.

STEP 3:

Discovering Your Color

When it comes to color, follow your heart. That simple piece of advice works, once you discover your color preferences. Color preferences are not always the same as favorite colors. You may love cobalt blue as glass—but not as a color on your walls. Lightened and subdued, cobalt might become a color you'd like to live with, a color you prefer.

An idea file can help you identify your color preferences. Start with decorating books, magazines, and catalogs. Magazines are an excellent source of ideas because they reflect the latest color trends, yet they are inexpensive enough to cut up without guilt. Designer showhouses are another great resource because they feature complete rooms, with the latest ideas for everything from furniture to light fixtures and wall coverings.

As you look through your books and magazines, flag or cut out pictures of things that appeal to you, whether it's an entire room, a fabric, or a vase of flowers. Do colored walls look inviting? Do you like the feel of an all-white room? Do you prefer florals or textured solids? Don't try to analyze why you like something; just collect the ideas. Include family members in this discovery process, because everyone's preferences count.

To begin to analyze your color preferences, sit down with your idea file and ask yourself a few questions. Start with color itself:

- Do you like cool blues, greens, and violets? Or warm reds, yellows, and oranges? Turn to the color rings on pages 11–13 to see the possibilities. Perhaps you feel more at ease with neutrals (pages 14–15).

- Do you prefer combinations of just a few colors, or combinations that include many colors? One approach is not necessarily easier than the other; it's all a matter of taste.

- Which is your least-favorite color? For adults, it's usually orange. But, can you see the potential in light-value, low-intensity versions of orange, colors that might be described as apricot or spice? In the right form, in the right amount, and in the right situation, your least-favorite color may turn out to be just right. Don't rule it out.

- Do you prefer light, airy colors or dark, dramatic ones? Bright colors or quiet colors? Recognizing your preferences in these aspects of color is especially helpful when you choose wall color.

- What part of the natural world appeals to you? Just because you love the ocean doesn't mean you must build your color scheme around blue—in

ABOVE: *A child's room is a great place to have fun with color, lots of color. Kids' preferences tend toward high-intensity hues.*

fact, ocean colors include many warm hues. But your preference might lead you to blue-greens, yellow-greens, even yellow-oranges, as well as neutrals.

- Do you long for a calm space, or do you hope to create a high-energy room? If you favor a quiet ambience, use neutrals, a single color in many variations, or related colors, such as cool blues and violets or warm apricots and yellows. If you're after excitement, opt for more contrast—colors from all around the color ring, lots of light/dark contrast, and doses of high-intensity color.

Remember: color preferences change over a lifetime. They also shift based on what's shown; as opinionated as we think we are, we learn to like what we see. It's an advantage to be drawn to current colors because you'll have more choices when you gather samples.

Preferences

COLOR CUE

As you gather, keep in mind that color on a paint chip or fabric sample will seem much more intense when it's applied to walls or furnishings.

■

LEFT: Contemporary chairs exemplify design simplicity and suggest a lead fabric with similar shapes and colors (below) and a cast of supporting materials (right).

STEP 4:

Armed with your wish list, a sketch of your room, and your color preferences, you're ready to gather materials. If you're feeling overwhelmed, relax. Hunting and gathering is all about possibilities, not final decisions, and it's meant to be fun. Imagine yourself shopping in preparation for a special meal. Just as a cook needs a recipe and the freshest ingredients, you need a decorating plan and wonderful materials to work with.

If you've come this far, you may have noticed that you have not yet chosen colors for a "color palette." That's the way it should be. Cast a wide net at this stage and simply gather what you love.

Give yourself plenty of time to gather. Like all

things in life, it will take longer than you think. You won't find everything on your first outing, and your ideas will surely evolve as you go. Don't push yourself; allow the process to become a pleasure.

Your inclination may be to gather in a methodical fashion. Perhaps you find a fabric you think would look great on a chair; then you cart it around as you search for fabric, carpet, tile, or paint that "goes." It's fine to have a starting point, but unless you're working with a fabulous given, try to avoid the one-thing-at-a-time approach. Color usually happens all at once, and at this stage you can just gather, without a firm idea of what goes where. That comes later. When you work this way, you are, in effect, starting *everywhere*.

Choose things that, in and of themselves, are beautiful. Don't settle for the first thing you see—unless it's irresistible—and don't try to make do with a fabric or wallpaper just to save money or time. If you don't like it now, you won't like it later, and you'll always be sorry you chose it.

Where do you gather? Paint stores, fabric stores, furniture stores, department stores, lighting centers, home centers, and interior design firms hold a wealth of inspiration.

If you live in or near a large city that has a professional design center, be sure to visit. Most design centers admit the public; to take

Hunting & Gathering

home "memo samples" or order materials or furnishings, though, you'll need to go through an interior designer.

In the showrooms you will encounter every material imaginable, from fabrics and furniture to tile and rugs. Many make a point of being trendy, so don't be put off if you don't see your look. Identifying what you dislike can be just as important as discovering what you love. Wherever you go, try to set aside preconceived notions about color and open your eyes to fresh experience. Think of it as traveling to a foreign country—you're there to notice everything.

Don't be timid about gathering samples. It's better to consider a dozen fabrics than three. Later, you'll edit your samples, keeping the ones that work and setting aside the others. Your samples might include:

- fabric
- paint chips
- wallpaper
- carpet
- wood
- stone
- tile

TOP: You'll often find congenial fabrics grouped by common colors at home-decorating stores.

BOTTOM: A pleasing array of materials includes fabrics that vary in pattern style and scale, as well as compatible paint chips and trims.

ABOVE: A needlepoint pillow and ginger jar display one of the freshest and most popular color combinations.

Collect the largest possible samples of the materials you're considering. Paint chips and strips are too small for making final decisions, but you should still pick up every one that appeals to you. When you have the choice, opt for the largest possible chips. Many paint manufacturers offer color palette cards and brochures. (See "A Favorite Paint Color," page 51.)

Fabric stores will often cut generous samples of fabric for you. If not, buy the smallest cut, usually 1/4 yard. When you're evaluating fabrics, don't be afraid to unfurl the bolts, drape the fabric, and step back. This is your chance to see the way a fabric catches light, and how it might look on a chair or at a window. Check how several fabrics look together. Store managers don't mind, and you'll have a better visual memory when you begin to edit your gathered samples.

Many stores and design firms allow you to borrow wallpaper books, samples of fabric, and tile, carpet, and other flooring samples. You can usually keep the samples for several days. For materials you can't check out, you'll need to bring your other samples with you to see how they look together.

Some furniture stores have in-house designers who will help you choose the fabric, as well as the frame and details, for an upholstered piece. Many also have computers that can show at a glance how a particular fabric will look on a piece of furniture you're considering.

If, after a day or two of gathering, you feel like the victim of sensory overload, remember: you aren't required to use everything you collect. Your goal is to gather a group of visually appealing samples that inspire and delight you. No commitments, not yet.

If you don't have the time to hunt and gather, enlist the help of an interior designer. They know the territory. Even if you're doing it all yourself, you may want to set up a one- or two-hour consultation with a designer. (Ask friends for a recommendation or call the regional chapter of the American Society of Interior Designers.) A designer can make suggestions, which you are free to implement on your own. A designer can also direct you to stores or showrooms he or she thinks you will like, cutting down on the time you spend in the search. A few hours' consultation with a good designer at the start of a project is a wise investment.

TOP: If possible, unroll fabrics to see the full effect of their patterns and textures. And, by all means, stand back.
BOTTOM: Satisfying—and sometimes surprising—combinations are more likely to develop when you keep everything in view.

STARTING POINTS

■

TOP LEFT: A fabric with abstract roses is the color catalyst for a pretty palette. When your scheme is limited to just two colors, variations in pattern and texture become even more important.

TOP RIGHT: Patterned, striped, and sheer fabrics key off a neutral black-and-brown fabric, illustrating the principle that unmatched materials are usually more intriguing than matching ones.

MIDDLE LEFT: A solid key fabric (center) can suggest other fabrics in similar or related colors. Repeat patterns and textures for a sense of visual rhythm.

MIDDLE RIGHT: The checkered fabric was the start for an analogous collection. Variations in value, scale, pattern, and texture make the scheme seem more complex.

BOTTOM LEFT: A richly patterned key fabric (center) in low-intensity reds and greens inspired a diverse gathering of materials, including stone.

BOTTOM RIGHT: Creamy whites and new neutrals display a sophisticated range of patterns, textures, and finishes. The stylized floral fabric (center) was the starting point.

Gathering lots of different samples is a great way to develop a decorating plan because it exposes you to new colors, materials, and ideas. You may, however, already have a fabulous fabric, a special rug, or a favorite paint color that you'd like to use as a starting point. That's fine. Following are guidelines for creating winning combinations.

A KEY FABRIC

Fabric is a popular and comfortable starting point for novices. Considering fabric first is a sound approach if you're planning to paint because it's relatively easy to find paint colors that work with your chosen fabrics and other materials.

Don't limit yourself to one key fabric; instead, work with several. As you find supporting materials, you'll quickly see which fabric has the most potential.

What makes a great key fabric? Above all else, it should be a fabric that you love. Starting with anything less is a mistake; you can never build a great scheme from a so-so piece of fabric. One that contains more rather than fewer colors gives you the most options.

Working with a multicolored key fabric has advantages and pitfalls. On the plus side, a key fabric provides a ready–made palette of pleasing colors. In effect, the fabric designer has done the creative work for you.

The disadvantage to starting with a key fabric is that you may be tempted to search for materials that match the colors in your fabric. That's usually a mistake. Even if you find an exact match, the material may not be harmonious with the other materials. Instead, seek out colors that blend, such as a red that is a bit warmer than the red-violet in your key fabric.

To help you find compatible (but not matching) materials, look at your key fabric from a distance, across the room. A green fabric with a yellow design may appear olive when you stand back; that's because your eye mixes the colors to make a new color, yellow-green. Try introducing a fabric in this perceived color, even though it doesn't exist in your key fabric.

You can also use a solid as your key fabric, as long as it's beautiful. Starting with a solid fabric forces you to create an original scheme, one that's inspired by your personal color preferences. Monochromatic and analogous schemes (page 16) can be easy or difficult to pull together, depending on the materials you find when you shop. Complementary and complex schemes (page 17) require more courage, but they can also be more striking because they include colors from different parts of the color ring.

COLOR CUE

Nowhere is it written that you must use a key fabric in your room. If it inspires you or leads you in a new direction, it has served its purpose.

STARTING POINTS

A SPECIAL RUG

If you have an heirloom rug as one of your givens, or if you plan to start with a new rug, you will probably want to build your scheme around it. Take your inspiration from the colors in the rug, but remember: it's not desirable to match colors. A little dissonance is more appealing than an over-coordinated look. And, as with a key fabric, it's not necessary to use all of the rug colors in your scheme. Use only the ones that appeal to you and that work well together.

Start by making a list of the colors. This list may be quite long, depending on the design. Obviously, it's not feasible to carry a rug with you when you hunt and gather, so take a few pictures before you begin. You won't get perfect color rendition, but photos can help you better remember the colors.

Collect materials just as you would with a key fabric, but avoid the trap of "pulling" an accent color from your rug and using it too prominently in your room. Just because blue appears as a speck in your rug doesn't mean you should use a similar blue on a chair or sofa.

If your rug has an open, airy background, try to determine its undertones (pages 22–23) and choose a wall color with similar undertones. If the rug's background is apricot, for example, a paint with orange undertones will be harmonious. It's just as important to choose a wall color of similar intensity. A clear color on your walls may not work if the background color in your rug is muted.

Throughout the process, try to imagine how your rug will relate to the floor, walls, and furnishings. Once you've gathered samples, bring them to your rug and begin the editing process (pages 58–61). Be sure to do brush-outs (pages 64–65) to see potential paint colors with your rug.

LEFT: A Tibetan rug inspired a far-ranging collection of samples, some of them a bit surprising.
BELOW: Winnow your samples to include materials whose colors and values echo—but do not necessarily match—the colors and values in the rug.

A FAVORITE PAINT COLOR

Starting with paint is more challenging than starting with a fabric, but you can do it, and do it well, if you're patient and persistent. You may feel at a disadvantage working this way, with limited options. Actually, it can be liberating when paint is the first material chosen, like a given, because it provides you with a strong color direction and narrows down your choices. And if your walls are already painted, you don't need to imagine how they might look, which makes the editing and auditioning process (pages 58–61) that much easier.

If you plan to start with paint but haven't yet chosen a color, take the time to look at painted walls in books, magazines, and homes to find your color comfort zone.

A paint sample board is a useful hunting-and-gathering tool. A short piece of molding—short enough to tuck into a tote bag—works well. Prime the molding to get the truest color; then paint a band of each color on the board, including paint for the ceiling and the trim. Take this board with you when you search for samples.

Choose materials whose colors are congenial with your paint colors, but avoid the temptation to match. Matching other materials to paint is an exercise in futility, and compatible colors are always more interesting than perfect matches.

Some paint companies offer palette cards and brochures, and you can make them work for you in the same way as a key fabric. (These palettes are different from paint strips, which typically show a light-to-dark range of values of a single color.) If you've chosen your paint colors from a palette card or brochure, use the remaining colors in other ways. A color that might be described as "espresso" on a palette card could be the perfect hue for an area rug; a color called "biscotti" on the same card might be just right for your window treatments or sofa.

TOP: *Paint brochures and palette cards provide ready–made combinations.*

ABOVE AND LEFT: *A paint color or colors can lead you to fabrics in related hues. If you choose wisely, the paint will look like an integral part of your decorating plan.*

Whether you realize it or not, your personal palette naturally develops as you gather samples. Take a look at how a palette might evolve from hunting and gathering, and how additions might improve it.

Imagine that your color preferences include a deep red-orange that is best described as terra-cotta. In hunting and gathering, you found mugs and dishes in some colors you like, including terra-cotta.

While browsing the bolts at the fabric store, you spot a paisley fabric that is predominantly red-orange, with accent colors of green, orange, yellow-orange, and red. You like the classic look of the fabric, so you ask for a swatch and begin to search for harmonious materials.

A few bolts away, you see a dark terra-cotta chenille in a large-scale leaf pattern, with subtle green and peach in the background. This fabric repeats some of the paisley colors and adds a rich texture.

Next you discover another chenille, this one a light orange that might be described as "cantaloupe," with russet outlines. Another textured fabric in warm colors comes into the mix.

So far, the dominant colors in your fabrics are all warm, and you begin to think about adding cooler hues. Green is an obvious choice because it appears in two of your fabrics. The green in the paisley is cool, almost aqua, while the green in the terra-cotta chenille is a warm sage. Across the store, you spot a low-intensity green fabric with a large-scale, swirling pattern. The swirls read as a cool green, the background a warm, nearly neutral gold.

Bolt by bolt, your palette evolves and becomes richer and more diverse, far beyond your original simple preference for terra-cotta. A peach-and-red silk lightens the palette. Additional greens cool down the warm hues. A few redder reds, including one fabric with yellow-gold dots, prove that "wandering around the color ring" (page 11) is a good way to push a scheme beyond the predictable. Warm woods and wall colors echo the colors in the fabrics and round out the palette.

Gathering samples and developing a palette are simultaneous steps, and the process is seamless. When you gather, let your preferences guide you, but stay open to the possibilities.

At some point, difficult as it is, you must stop gathering and evaluate what you've collected. Ask yourself some questions.

- Where do the colors in your materials fall on the color ring? Don't think about adding colors at this point; just note where yours are. In this example, terra-cotta (red-orange) and sage (yellow-green) are almost opposite on the color ring. Peach—a light value of orange—and red lie on either side of red-orange.

- Look at your gathered samples as a group. What kind of color combination do they form? Your combination will fit, or be similar to, one of the four schemes on pages 16–17. (A neutral scheme is the exception because neutrals don't appear on the color rings; see pages 14–15.) Here, it's roughly complementary because the colors are approximately opposite.

- Using what you know about color combinations, can you gather more samples to complete your palette? In this example, the green fabrics balance the visual temperature.

As you work with your samples to develop your palette, keep everything in the running. In the next step, "Editing and Auditioning" (pages 58–61), you'll begin to winnow down your materials and fine-tune your palette.

It can be difficult, especially if you're new to working with color, to envision a well-developed palette. For examples of professional palettes, turn to pages 134-141. Notice where the colors fall on the mini color rings; see how value and intensity vary among the painted colors. To use one of these palettes in your home, gather materials in the colors shown and consider the suggestions for placement. You are free, of course, to "edit" any one of these palettes to fit your decorating plan.

Your Palette

The collection (left) coordinates itself. From top, left to right, it consists of: red-orange paisley; terra-cotta chenille; cantaloupe chenille; green velvet swirl; peach-and-red silk; green silks; red silks; wood, wallpaper, stone, and paint.

COLOR CUE

Remember that color occurs in materials other than fabric. In a room with a palette of red, yellow, and blue, maple or oak floors can be one version of yellow.

PATTERN & TEXTURE

All materials possess pattern and texture, qualities that give color much of its visual character. The principles that follow are intended to guide you as you gather, edit, and try out your materials, but they are not rules. Look through any decorating magazine and you will see rooms that defy these guidelines, with great results. The novice might want to be a bit more cautious.

PATTERN

Many people experience "pattern panic" when they attempt to choose and combine patterns. A familiarity with pattern will ease your anxiety and help you combine patterns with confidence. Although we tend to associate pattern with fabrics, keep in mind that it occurs in all kinds of materials, including wallpaper, carpeting, wood grain, and tile.

Pattern Scale

The size of the motifs or design lines in a pattern is known as scale. Scale is usually described as small, medium, or large.

Small-scale patterns. These tend to read as textured or solid from a distance. Use them with solids, or as visual relief among other patterns.

Medium-scale patterns. These are more versatile because they retain their design, even from a distance, yet rarely overpower other patterns. You can easily use them with small- and large-scale patterns.

Large-scale patterns. Choose these with care; they look even bolder on furnishings or made up into window treatments. A large-scale pattern may look fragmented on a small piece of furniture.

TOP RIGHT: *Changes in the scale of patterns affect the way we perceive color in fabrics.*

MIDDLE RIGHT: *Simple dots and stripes in related (but not matching) colors complement a realistic floral pattern.*

BOTTOM RIGHT: *Patterns have both actual (tactile) and visual (perceived) texture, ranging from smooth to rough.*

RIGHT: Patterns of vastly different scale are compatible when they contain common colors. A checked floor adds a different kind of pattern to the mix.

BELOW: Stripes, florals, and toiles (realistic depictions of country life) illustrate a principle of pattern mixing: repeat colors, while varying the style and scale of the patterns.

Pattern Style

If you're not familiar with the pattern possibilities, prepare to be surprised—and maybe even a little overwhelmed—when you hunt and gather. Patterns range from realistic depictions of nature, most commonly flowers and leaves, to abstract designs, stripes, dots, and plaids. To familiarize yourself with what's available, browse through the samples at fabric and furniture stores or look through decorating books and magazines. Fabric ads are a great resource because they show the fabrics up close.

PATTERN & TEXTURE

Pattern Combinations

Strive to combine patterns that are different enough to be interesting, yet similar enough to be harmonious. Sound complicated? It's not. Following are a few tips.

- Base your pattern decisions on what's happening with your walls and floor. If they are solid or near-solid, such as plain painted walls, wood floors, or near-solid carpet, you can easily use three patterns in your room without overload.

- Vary the patterns for interest. To a plaid, you might add a pattern with curves. Naturalistic patterns, such as florals, combine well with stripes.

- Strive for a similar theme among your patterns. A small, delicate floral won't work with a rugged Italian tapestry, but a jacquard probably will.

- Vary the scale as well as the pattern—but not too much. To a floral with 5-inch motifs, for example, you might add a 3-inch plaid. An oversized pattern and a miniprint may look incompatible together.

ABOVE: Shiny and matte, smooth and nubby—textures are every bit as important as color in a successful scheme. Solid colors show off interesting textures best.

BELOW: Diverse patterns, textures, and finishes—including metallic wallpaper, give visual interest, while new–neutral colors convey a sense of calm.

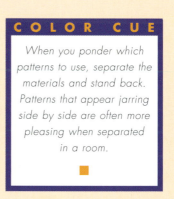

- If you combine too many patterns, the effect can be chaotic. Try to create places for the eye to rest by including solid colors or subtly textured materials among patterns.

- Distribute patterns throughout a room for a pleasing visual rhythm. Clustering patterned materials can make a room look lopsided.

- Unite different patterns with a common characteristic, such as a similar pink in a floral, stripe, and plaid.

Strive for harmony when you combine patterns, just as you would when choosing colors. Be willing to edit patterned materials as necessary.

TEXTURE

Texture affects our perception of color, perhaps even more so than pattern, yet it is often overlooked when choosing materials. Nubby silk, polished wood, slick stainless steel, smooth tile, and reedy wicker are just a few examples of textures you will encounter in the marketplace.

Texture modulates color in powerful ways. Textured materials such as tapestry have tiny peaks and valleys that absorb rather than reflect light, lowering the intensity of the color. Texture also affects value: colors on shiny surfaces appear to be lighter, colors on more textured materials darker. Yellow silk pillows will look lighter than a corduroy chair upholstered in the same yellow.

Combining textures, like combining patterns, is a balancing act. Here are three simple guidelines.

- Use a variety of textures, just as you would patterns. Toss a pebbly knit throw on a leather sofa, or mix linen and chintz in a room. Exercise some restraint, however; too much texture can be visually confusing.
- Make texture an essential element in a neutral or monochromatic scheme. Smooth silk and textured damask in the same color are pleasing together because they have different textures.
- When you're working with more than one color, unite them with similar textures, such as glistening wood and shimmery silk in a dining room, or a thick braided rug and a twill chair in a family room.

ABOVE: Common colors unite dramatically different patterns, textures, and materials.
BELOW: "Elephant-skin" wallpaper with a bronze overlay shares wall space with a classic mural. Creams, taupes, and black make up the new-neutral palette used here.

COLOR CUE

The effects of texture make it nearly impossible to match colors in different materials, such as carpet, fabric, and paint. Besides, it's more interesting if the colors have a controlled element of surprise.

STEP 6: Editing and

Finally it's time to choose materials and decide where to place them in your room. This step is probably the most exciting, but it can also be the most intimidating. If making decisions makes you nervous, relax. When you choose appealing materials, you're sure to come up with a plan that pleases you. Take it slowly and enjoy the process and the possibilities.

Spread out your samples on a large surface such as your dining room table or pin them to a large bulletin board or piece of foam-core board. Plan to leave them there as long as it takes—that could mean days or weeks. Accept the clutter and enjoy the blend of colors and textures. If you must return borrowed samples in a few days, however, you'll need to work more quickly.

Your inclination, with a sea of samples in front of you, is to freeze. So many materials, so many choices! Stay open, and let the ideas percolate. Casually glance at your table every time you pass by; study your samples when you have more time. Encourage family members to do likewise.

Don't rush this step—your feelings may change as you see your materials over time and under different light. It may make you feel better to know that interior designers check out many memo samples from showrooms and never use most of them. Gather more samples, using your preferences and your palette as guides, if you feel constrained by what you have. Hunting and gathering often continue to the very end.

ABOVE LEFT: Coloring your room sketch (see "Assessing Your Space," pages 40–41) can help you audition colors and materials.

ABOVE: Light-value, low-intensity red-orange, a color that might be described as terra-cotta, is ideal for large furnishings, where more intense colors might overpower. Yellow-orange plaster walls (the color is integral, not painted on) harmonize with color-washed pine and a new-neutral green carpet. The darker, more intense fabrics are effective as pillows.

RIGHT: A harmonious group of edited materials is both varied and unified. Low-intensity red, red-orange, green, and yellow-green, approximately opposite on the color ring, are subtle and sophisticated; warm gold expands the scheme. Intriguing patterns, textures, and finishes modulate the colors.

Some obvious questions will arise as you begin the winnowing process.

- "Do I truly love what I see?" If you chose samples and developed your palette according to your color preferences, what you see in front of you will please you. Resist the temptation to keep a material you think you should include but don't especially like, such as a drab fabric that seems to bridge the gap between two dissimilar fabrics. You'll never like it, so eliminate it now.

- "Do I have too much of one thing?" If you've collected three black-and-cream stripes or four variations of teal, now is the time to select one or two and set the others aside. Keep them in peripheral view, however, because you may later reconsider and decide to return a rejected material to the mix.

- "Is there too much contrast?" Sharply contrasting values—light lights and dark darks—make a strong statement. It's easiest to use similar but not identical values, such as a range of medium colors. Remember that neutrals—an off-white paint for trim, for example, or black lighting fixtures—will also add contrast.

- "Are my samples too subdued?" To play it safe, you may have unconsciously chosen all low-intensity colors; they just seem to "go together." You may, in fact, prefer a subdued, simple palette, such as all white or all beige. But unless that's your goal, try including a few brighter notes.

Auditioning

COLOR CUE

It's essential to view your collected samples together, as a group, because that's how they will appear in your room. With color, context is critical.

- "Do I have a good mix of patterns and textures?" Too much pattern or texture leads to visual chaos; not enough can make a room look incomplete. Review the guidelines in "Pattern and Texture" (pages 54–57).
- "Do I need more of one color, or another color?" Consider adding more of one color or a new color altogether if you feel that your palette is skimpy. To spark new ideas, review "Color Combinations" (pages 16–17). Sometimes the best color, the one that really makes a scheme come to life, is the least obvious.

Throughout the editing process, think of harmony and balance. Looking at your samples, nothing should jump out or jar your senses.

The hardest step—deciding what goes where—comes next. Take another look at the materials on your table, this time with an eye toward placement. Perhaps you envision the khaki solid on the sofa, the small green-and-gray print on a club chair, the neutral sheer at the windows. Now is the time to audition those ideas in your room.

As much as possible, study your samples where you anticipate using them. Place flooring samples on the floor, next to your brush-outs (pages 64–65). Prop up wallpaper books across the room and stand back to see the effect. If you have large pieces of fabric, drape them over your furniture. Fold potential pillow fabrics and place them on top of other fabrics. Scrunch up a window-treatment fabric to see how it might appear in gathers or pleats. In other words, let your room "try on" your samples.

As you review your materials, think about how much of each color you plan to use. In general, the larger the area, the bolder a color will appear. A red that's subdued on a pillow will look strong on your sofa, and much stronger on your walls. When it comes to color, amount is everything. Interior designers suggest that you use low-intensity color on large areas or furnishings and intense color on smaller areas. They sometimes break this rule, but it's still a helpful guideline when deciding whether to choose a true orange or cinnamon (a dark, low-intensity version of orange) for your sofa.

If you're brave enough to select intense colors for large areas, get the largest possible samples and consider them carefully before making decisions. And remember: we tire of intense colors quickly—that's why

COLOR CUE

Retail-store lighting, which is usually fluorescent, is different from the lighting in your home, which is usually a mix of incandescent and natural light. That's why it's important to try out samples in your home.

■

*LEFT: From upstairs to down-
stairs, the wall color shifts
from yellow-orange to rosy
terra-cotta. A slightly different
carpet, also new-neutral
green, and pine baseboards
visually link the spaces.*

*RIGHT: In the same home, a
bathroom adjoining the living
room illustrates the quiet
power of color carried from
room to room. A concrete
countertop and backsplash in
new-neutral gray-green echo
the color of the living room
carpet. Golden yellow traver-
tine repeats, with slight variation, the wall color.*

people tend to use them in small quantities. It's easy to buy a new pillow, but not so easy to recover your sofa.

Distribute the colors in your palette throughout the room or rooms. If you're doing several rooms, you might use your main colors in one room, and one or two of the colors in adjoining rooms. Don't use a color just once in a room: it may grab your attention or, worse, look like a mistake.

If you're having trouble visualizing the possibilities, it may be time to revisit your idea file. Do you like dark walls? What does it look like to have a bright red chair, instead of one that's subdued? Do you really want a blue sofa? A return visit to the sources of your samples may also be in order. Showrooms and furniture stores are good places to get a sense of how colors will appear in your home.

Making the leap from trying out your samples to actually buying materials is perhaps the most difficult step in the process. Everyone wants to be happy with the outcome, and no one wants to make a mistake. But if you've come this far, you should have the confidence to go ahead. At every stage, ask yourself, "Do these colors make my heart sing?" "Is the effect harmonious and balanced?" "Will I feel truly at home living in this room?" If you've edited and auditioned your samples well, you'll answer yes to all three.

WHEN WE THINK OF COLOR IN THE HOME, MOST OF US
THINK OF PAINTED WALLS. PAINT HAS THE POWER TO TRANSFORM A ROOM.
AND OF ALL THE HOME DECORATING PROJECTS YOU MIGHT
UNDERTAKE, PAINTING IS PROBABLY # Color and **PAINT**
THE EASIEST TO DO YOURSELF.

LEFT AND BELOW: Yellow-orange paint illuminates the space and turns a well-put-together room (below) into a sensational one (left), tying together colors, patterns, and textures.

PAINT BASICS

It matters which type of paint you choose because a paint's finish affects color. Popular paint finishes include matte, eggshell, pearl, satin, semigloss, and gloss. Matte paints absorb light rather than reflect it, creating flat, opaque color. Glossy paints reflect maximum light. In general, the higher the gloss, the lighter, more intense the color rendition.

Here are some guidelines to help you succeed with paint.

- Paint always looks stronger on walls than on paint chips. What appears to be gray with just a hint of violet on a paint chip may look purple on your walls. In general, a color on a paint chip will look one

or two values darker on your walls. That's why it's important to do brush-outs (pages 64–65).

- Paint palette cards and brochures (page 51) group congenial colors, sometimes by theme, such as "canyon lands" or "safari." A theme palette is a great tool because the colors are varied yet have something in common, such as a similar intensity or similar undertones, that makes them harmonious.
- When adjoining rooms are painted different colors, use the same trim color to visually link the spaces. Variations of white are most common, other colors more adventuresome.
- Feel free to use different colors on molding, baseboards, frames, and casings, especially if these features are architecturally noteworthy. You might, for example, use one trim color on crown molding and window frames and a different color on baseboards and door casings.
- Wainscoting provides an opportunity to use more than one paint color. For a quiet effect, use a light color on the wainscoting and a darker value of the same color on the wall.
- The same color will look darker on the ceiling than on the walls, due to differences in the way light hits adjoining surfaces.
- A kitchen, which often has little wall space, is an ideal place to experiment with stronger color. So is a stairwell or a powder room.
- Painting a great room a single color is the most common approach. If you choose to break up the space with different colors on different walls, such as one color on the fireplace wall and another on a window wall, plan carefully and do side-by-side brush-outs. Be aware, however, that you'll need sharp, clean edges for abutting colors, or molding that marks their division.

Decorative paint finishes rely on the interplay and layering of colors for their intriguing visual effects. A preference for using decorative paint rather than traditional wallpaper reflects the desire for a crafted rather than mass-produced look. (Ironically, newer wallpapers often mimic decorative paint finishes.) Consider these finishes when you want rich, complex color with the illusion of texture, depth, and movement. Decorative finishes that involve layers of subtle color can visually unite a scheme in a way not always possible with a single paint color.

TOP: Very light-value, low-intensity colors with warm and cool undertones illustrate the calming influence of paint.
BOTTOM: Walls painted a high-energy blue-violet are tempered by handpainted tile, copper accents, and warm wood.

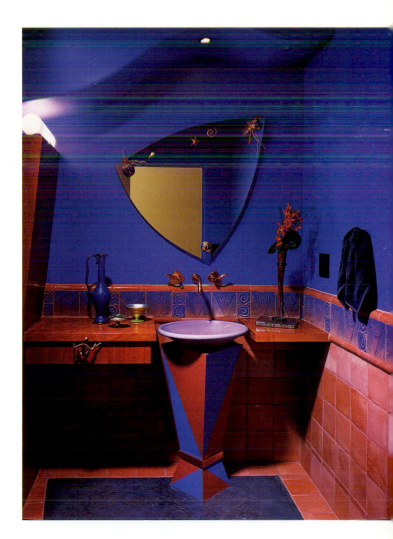

TOP LEFT: *Dining room fabrics include warm gold (a dark value of yellow) and yellow-greens, with roughly complementary violets and red-violets.*

LOWER LEFT: *Reds and yellow-oranges key off a richly textured rug for the living room.*

BELOW, TOP: *A brush-out in the hallway shows how different the same paint color looks on walls and ceiling. A deeper, darker color is tested on the ceiling of the room beyond.*

BELOW, BOTTOM: *As you look from one room to another, brush-outs show how potential paint colors might look together.*

BRUSH-OUTS

"Brush-out" is the term interior designers and painters use to describe the equivalent of test-driving paint. Take the time to do brush-outs; it's the only way to accurately predict how color will look on your walls. Plan to test three or four colors for the first round, more if necessary. It's not uncommon for a designer to test six versions of taupe to find just the right color.

It can be difficult to choose paint color, and paint strips certainly don't make it easier. But you must begin somewhere. Start with the chips, strips, palette cards, or brochures you picked up while hunting and gathering. Individual chips or palette cards that contain three or four colors are less confusing than strips with six to eight colors.

If you must choose from a strip with a range of values, zero in on a color somewhere in the middle of the strip. The tendency is to go with a light color, out of fear, but a mid-value color has more character. Remember, brush-outs aren't permanent, and you can always go lighter later.

LEFT: *Looking at samples is one thing; seeing it all come together is another. What appeared to be very different materials at the hunting-and-gathering stage become a beautiful blend of warm color and rich pattern and texture.*

BELOW: *After painting, but before the furnishings fill the room, color looks its strongest.*

Brush-outs intimidate first-time painters because they seem to be time-consuming and costly, but paint is relatively inexpensive, and, if you're going to paint your walls, you'll paint over the brush-outs anyway. You might as well do large samples; a large brush-out gives you the best idea of how a color will look and be affected by the light, and if the color doesn't work, you'll soon cover it with one that does. You might prefer to do your brush-outs on pieces of plasterboard or foam-core board to allow you to move them around the room.

You can do brush-outs in several ways.

- Paint a large square or rectangle on one wall.
- Paint a wide strip from floor to ceiling, extending it onto the ceiling.
- Paint a corner, covering parts of each wall and the ceiling.

The second approach shows you how a potential wall color will look with your flooring, if the flooring is a given. The third approach illustrates, often dramatically, how light affects color. The same color looks different on adjoining surfaces because each surface receives a different amount of light. If you do a brush-out in a corner, it may look as though you used three different paints. In general, the ceiling color will appear darker because it receives the least light. You can compensate for this effect by painting the ceiling a lighter value of the same color, or you can simply enjoy the slight variation.

Once you've done your brush-outs, stand back and block out the surrounding area with your hands, as if framing a picture, and squint. Be sure to look at your brush-outs at different times of the day, in natural and artificial light.

And finally, a reassuring word about color and paint: if you take the plunge and paint your walls a strong color, you may be so surprised by the effect that your impulse is to retreat to white or a familiar color. Don't. Once you add your furnishings, flooring, and window treatments, the wall color will become part of a bigger picture and assume a more subordinate role.

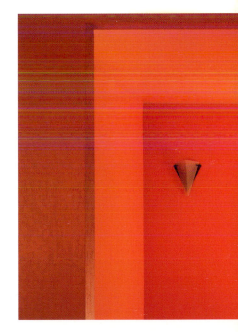

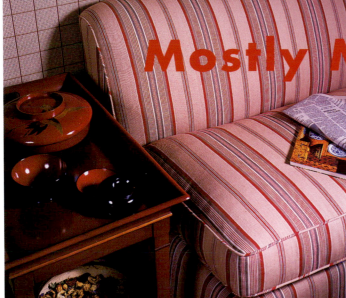

Mostly Monochromatic

LEFT: *A monochromatic scheme can include a wide range of light, creamy colors that function as neutrals. Repeat the starring color— red, in this living room—in furnishings and accessories.*

ABOVE: *Add interest to a one-color scheme by using a mix of solids and patterns.*

RIGHT: *A terra-cotta sofa and striped rug echo the look of the brick half-wall. When you work with one color, think of pattern and texture.*

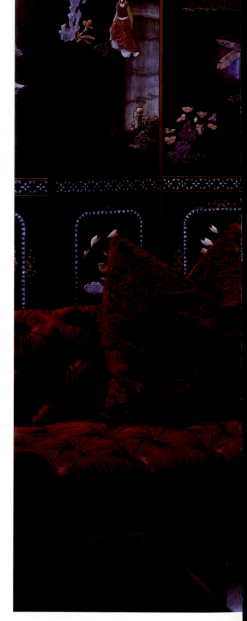

Asian Ambience

TOP LEFT: *A light glaze of celadon on a base of ivory creates the look of aged walls; a similar but slightly darker grayed green accentuates the molding and corner beam. Deep, dark woods and a multicolored slate floor balance the visual temperature.*

BOTTOM LEFT: *Glazed walls the color of platinum are meant to suggest the hues and textures of antique Japanese silk. Mossy green and neutral taupe exert a subtle cooling influence on the warm color.*

ABOVE: *High contrast and minimal color exemplify the Asian style. Smooth, shiny lacquer complements richly textured, deeply colored fabrics. Light-value walls tinged with green enhance the contrast.*

Bold, Brash Color

TOP RIGHT: *Surrounding bright colors with black makes them seem even more intense; the same colors against white wouldn't be as powerful.*

BOTTOM RIGHT: *In a sewing room stocked with quilting fabrics, yellow goes with everything. Intense yellow is ideal for walls because it is naturally light in value.*

ABOVE: *Who says you can't color-coordinate your toothbrushes with your tile?*

RIGHT: *Vibrant red, blue, and violet make a dramatic backdrop for equally colorful plates. Intense colors work well together because they "stand up" to one another.*

Blue and Green

BELOW: *Tile, tile everywhere, and most of it is green! Pink, yellow, and melon accents warm up the cool colors. Varying the quantities of color keeps a sense of calm.*

RIGHT: *A blue wall with green plates sets a decidedly cool mood, echoed in the playful floor. The key to success with cool color is just a hint of warmth, along the edges of this entry rug and in the yellow crockery in the kitchen to the right.*

LEFT: *Natural colors combine beautifully when the values are closely related and the textures are varied.*

BELOW: *Soft, powdery walls consist of a crackled over-glazing of white and cream on a background of taupe and umber. Gold-leaf molding marks the change in color from walls to ceiling.*

Lighten Up

LEFT: *Light walls, window treatments, and accessories set a romantic tone in a monochromatic room. Bits of color and pattern are subtle, yet essential, details.*

Serene Settings

ABOVE: *Intended as a lighthearted reference to the owner's abundant garden, this ethereal dining space features faux alabaster walls, a painted floorcloth, and a light fixture in the form of a metal vine.*
RIGHT: *Light values make a room seem calm and spacious. Warm tiles, counters, and floors balance minty green cabinets; the fresh red-violet tulips are a complementary accent.*

Warm Up to Color

BELOW: *Gleaming silk and nubby cotton fabrics, some handpainted in gold, have a similar visual temperature. Neutral sheers add pattern and texture.*

RIGHT: *Neutral, natural colors are warm and soothing. A rose-and-ecru chair repeats, on a much larger scale, the striped bed linen.*

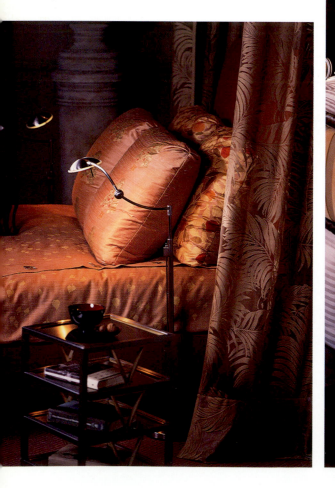

ABOVE: *Analogous peach (a light value of orange) and terra-cotta (a version of red-orange) bathe a powder room in warm color. A grayed blue in the painted screen adds a cool note.*

On the Green

ABOVE: White is the obvious choice for trim color in a monochromatic scheme. Plants repeat the green theme.

RIGHT: Greens of slightly different visual temperatures—warm green tile and cool green cabinetry—are unexpected yet harmonious. Red and other warm hues balance the cool colors.

FAR RIGHT: Glazed walls the color of clay are in stark contrast to green shutters and chairs. Sometimes too cool on its own, green almost always benefits from the presence of warmer hues.

LEFT: An intricately patterned rug suggests compatible colors in an eclectic study. The overall visual temperature is decidedly warm, with cool blue accents.

RIGHT: Yellow-greens and browns, including rich wood, envelop a dining room in warm color. Repeating analogous colors throughout is one way to unify a room.

BELOW: Elsewhere in the same room, another warm color, red, expands the scheme. Gold in the carpet and sofa links dramatically different patterns.

Warm Traditions

TOP LEFT: *A black ceiling and carpet frame walls the color of merlot, an earthy, umber red. Instead of lowering the ceiling, as dark colors are thought to do, black creates a sense of height and formality in this dining room. Breaking the ceiling with a border enhances the illusion.*

BOTTOM LEFT: *Stark color and value contrasts are favored in contemporary settings. Here, deep violet, terra-cotta, and red play against black.*

ABOVE: *In a palette made up of reds—including pink, a light value of red—and yellows, black plays a starring role. The elegant crown molding sets off a slightly darker ceiling. (See page 49, top right, for a photo of the materials.)*

Rich, Low-Key Color

Black Accents

LEFT: *Black and gray punctuate expanses of light value, low-intensity color in this offbeat bathroom. Slightly darker values of red and green add visual weight to the airy colors.*

ABOVE: *Black is an essential element in a mosaic floor composed of smashed tile shards. Solid-color walls are a visual respite from the highly patterned floor.*

ABOVE RIGHT: *Black lends itself to crisp geometric designs, offset here by whimsical painted walls.*

RIGHT: *Primary hues are ideal color companions for black; white provides a clean, simple backdrop.*

Painterly Effects

LEFT: *A favorite porcelain pattern inspired the graceful mural in this round dining room. Creamy white trim delineates panels painted a low-intensity green, with accents of equally subdued yellow, pink, and blue.*

ABOVE: *A trompe l'oeil transom is a playful, colorful addition to an airy solarium. Decorative paint effects are ideal for bringing unexpected color into a room.*

A dramatic space and striking view demand an equally bold color plan. Ebony hardwood floors reflect light coming through wide windows; a silver coating on the ceiling bounces light and draws attention upward. Walls painted a flat off-white play an important but supporting role.

Neutral Territory

Neutral Territory

RIGHT: Color, pattern, and texture are equal partners in a neutral room. Using materials whose undertones vary—even a little—expands a low-color scheme.

LEFT: Special effects, including decorative paint, gilt mirror, and iridescent fabric, make the most of a neutral palette.

RIGHT: *Neutrals lend themselves to lush textures and trims.*

LEFT: *Stark contrasts—black-and-white photos against gray walls—are less jarring in a true neutral scheme, where value is the main variable.*

New Neutrals

ABOVE: *Low-intensity greens—note that they do not match—function as new neutrals in a light-filled dining room. Slightly more intense yellow-orange walls and creamy trim make a glowing backdrop.*

LEFT: *A play of quiet color at the ceiling and just below draws attention upward. New neutrals almost always harmonize, especially if you repeat them or use them in similar ways.*

ABOVE RIGHT: *It's a fine line between colorful neutrals and neutralized color. Mustardy tile surrounds a gray—or is it green?—sink. Black serves as an accent.*

RIGHT: *The tile backsplash is a collage of new-neutral color. Countertops, a bamboo shade, even a pendant light fixture, add low-key color and texture.*

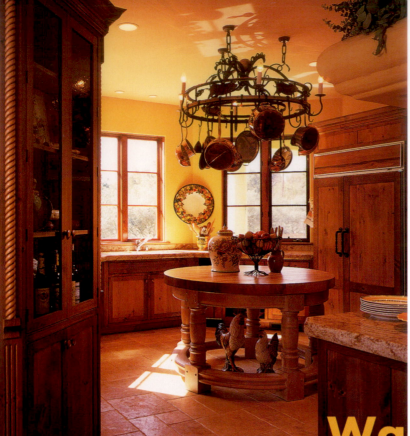

LEFT: *Warm walls, floors, and cabinetry make this sunny kitchen inviting. Although the colors come from the warm side of the color ring, the values vary from lights to darks.*

BELOW: *A kitchen, especially one with limited wall space, is a great place to use strong color. Yellow-orange tile and lamp shades are intensely warm; granite countertops and wood floors are more subdued. White cabinetry spaces out the color.*

RIGHT: *Dark wood cabinetry and stone flooring, both warm, are offset by cooler granite countertops. The brick is a neutral gray, warmed by task lighting.*

Warm Kitchens

ABOVE LEFT: *Light-value walls and medium-value furnishings and flooring are a recipe for harmony in a traditional scheme. The colors are related, but variations in value create a sense of greater contrast.*

LEFT: *A palette ranging from yellow through blue-green on the color ring looks more complex when the materials are varied. The gold tassels are just another version of yellow.*

ABOVE: *An analogous scheme of yellow, yellow-green, green, and blue-green is anything but dull, thanks to a vigorous mix of pattern and texture. Complementary red introduces an element of color surprise.*

Analogous Color

LEFT: *The homeowners' cats—one imperious, the other a known thief—inspired this real-life dumbwaiter. Low-intensity colors enhance the illusion.*

RIGHT: *Trompe l'oeil is a fanciful way to add color and pattern to a room. In the same home, on another dumbwaiter, Alice studies the magic door as the Cheshire cat looks on. Details in both pieces are taken from the homeowners' lives.*

BELOW: *Color, even in small doses, packs a powerful punch.*

Colorful Deceptions

Cooling Trends

BELOW: Wood painted a strong blue-green is a cool backdrop for warmer-colored furnishings, flooring, and window treatments. Carrying the color to the ceiling makes the room cozier.

RIGHT: Brilliant blue-green cushions punctuate a scheme of natural colors and textures. Warm neutrals almost always benefit from the cooling influence of green, blue-green, or blue.

BELOW RIGHT: A less-than-desirable given—old wall tile—became an asset with the help of decorative paint. Aqua and apple green, in combination with metallic copper and gold, create the look of verdigris.

TOP: Silvery fabric gathered on a rod takes the place of a closet door. Gold-leaf molding and silver paint carry out the old-world theme.

BOTTOM: A double-soffited ceiling features floral images in decorative paint; gold-, silver-, and copper-leaf finishes accentuate the unusual molding.

Special Effects

LEFT: *Luxurious-looking materials in this sumptuous bedroom include opalescent walls, handpainted fabrics, shimmery silks, art glass, and crystal beads.*

ABOVE: *Light plays off iridescent fabrics covering the window and rich fabrics on the pillows. The layering of materials enhances the visual effect.*

ABOVE: *Light- and medium-value versions of yellow, peach, and rose—all from the warm side of the color ring—unite disparate textures and finishes. Green pillows and pots are cooler notes.*

RIGHT: *Painting the ceiling a lighter, creamier color than the walls accentuates the sense of height in an elegant space. A simple window treatment, rod-pocket curtains, becomes glamorous when the fabric is striped silk.*

BELOW: *Near-whites and pale new neutrals with warm and cool undertones set a quiet mood.*

Creamy Color

LEFT: *Low color has high impact when the surfaces are intriguing. Venetian plaster walls and a barrel-vaulted ceiling stenciled with plaster are warm and neutral, while the cooktop and marble counters keep their cool.*

BELOW LEFT: *Pickled gray wood cabinetry is visually cool, as are appliances. Patterned chairs warm up the scheme.*

BELOW: *Cool marble becomes the focal point in this neutral kitchen. Gray trim is equally cool; the white cabinets are slightly warmer.*

RIGHT: *A burlap shade adds texture and neutral color to a pantry corner. Similar undertones in the wall color and window treatment keep the focus on an antique quilt.*

Low-Color Kitchens

LEFT: *Cobalt blue is anything but cold in the company of warm walls and wood finishes. Expressive accessories and imaginative fixtures offer even more opportunities to play with color.*

BELOW: *Chambray blue is no surprise on a sofa—but on the floor? Widely spaced stripes make blue the dominant hue in this triad (see page 17) of primaries. Red and yellow have a warming influence.*

RIGHT: *Bold patterns and low-intensity versions of red, yellow, and blue combine for a look that's both sophisticated and fun. Stripes on the chair, at the window, and in the concentric rug unify the room.*

Basic Blue

LEFT: Ocher yellow, rosy red, powdery red-orange, and grayed blue-green make up a colorful scheme, but without the edge of their intense counterparts. Contrasting piping accentuates the lines of subtly patterned furniture pieces; a custom rug ties it all together.

Harmonious Hues

ABOVE: Materials, as much as color, make this scheme succeed. Opalescent yellow walls with maple cabinets colorwashed in yellow bounce light in this contemporary bathroom. Gray and white marble, in contrast, is cool, as is the green-tinged glass basin.

LEFT: Grayed green and yellow paints create a simple pattern on a breakfast-nook bench. Plexiglass sconces, with brass backplates, were designed to age gracefully.

Checks and Balances

ABOVE: *Shared colors and a spirited mix of patterns and textures visually unite disparate fabrics and a handwoven rug.*

TOP RIGHT: *A palette of three colors—pale yellow, lime green, and orange sherbet—seems more complex because the values and intensities vary. These kindred colors all come from the warm side of the color ring.*

BOTTOM RIGHT: *Complementary pink and green are always pleasing when the colors are similar in value and intensity. This master bedroom and nursery illustrate the principles of pattern mixing: vary the pattern style and scale, while repeating colors.*

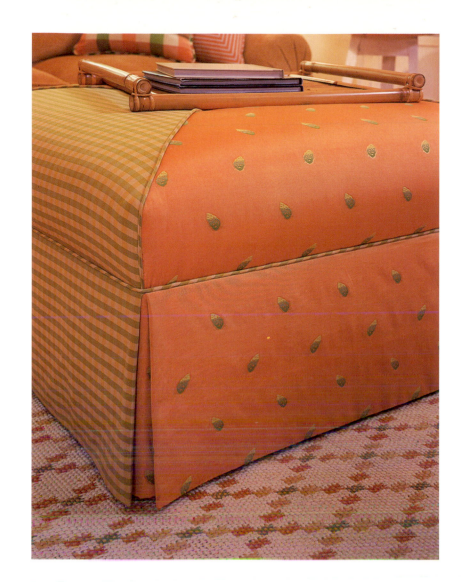

ABOVE: *A small-scale pattern, such as the blue-and-black check on these dining chairs, can soften the impact of high-intensity color. Pale yellow walls and natural cherry wood balance the cool blue; Italian glass tile adds other bits of color.*

RIGHT: *Full-intensity primaries are most effective when used in unequal quantities, as in the case of the accent provided by the cobalt blue pendant light.*

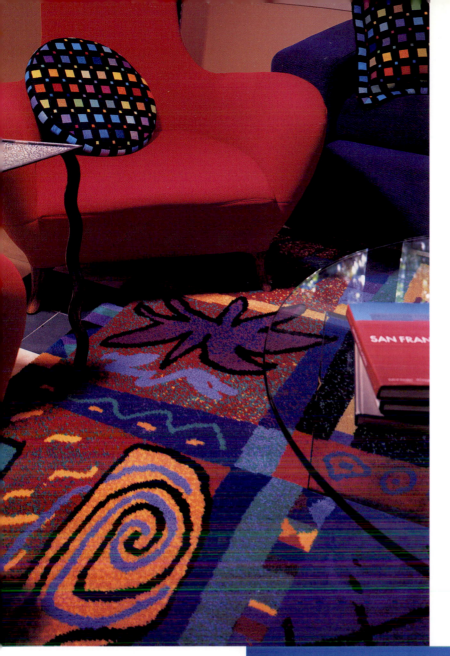

LEFT: *A bold area rug links patterned pillows and solid-color furnishings.*

BELOW: *High-energy color is right at home in a baby's room. The color-packed area rug includes red, yellow, and blue, plus green, a color commonly seen with primaries. Slightly less intense walls and furnishings tone down the strong hues.*

Color Is Primary

TOP LEFT: *Bullion fringe, which comes in a variety of sizes, colors, and fibers, offers a great opportunity to add color and texture to pillows and furnishings.*

BOTTOM LEFT: *Fanciful ceramic tassels make unusual tiebacks for window treatments.*

ABOVE: *A yellow-green-and-blue plaid fabric doesn't quite match the blue-green painted wood, but that's what makes this chair fresh.*

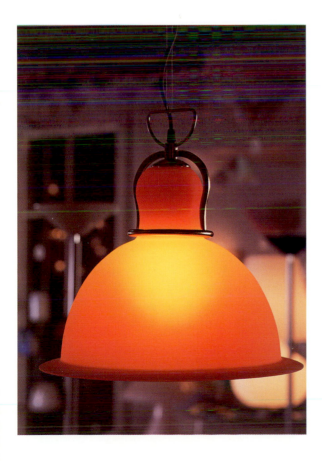

TOP LEFT: Never underestimate the power of quiet color, even in a small area. Varied hues harmonize because all are relatively low in intensity.

BOTTOM LEFT: Tinted glass light fixtures bring luminous color to a room.

BELOW: A jumble of mismatched pillows makes a comfortably casual color statement.

Details Count

APPENDIX: COLOR PALETTES

PALETTE #1

Complementary pink (a light value of red) and green are a perennial favorite. When you work with colors opposite on the color ring, choose low-intensity versions to soften the contrast. Varying the values, even a little, adds depth to a scheme. A near-white is ideal for walls.

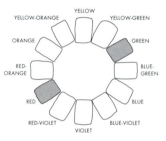

PALETTE #2

Low-intensity colors on the cool side of the color ring are related, yet different enough to be interesting. Violet, an effective bridging color (page 9), adds a little warmth to cool blue and green. A grayish green is a harmonious companion color.

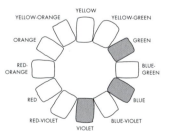

PALETTE #3

Blue-green and peach, near complements on the color ring, benefit from unexpected yellow-green. Coral (a light value of red-orange) stretches the scheme even farther and keeps it from looking like a color formula. Pale peach and soft yellow—both appropriate colors for walls or trim—lighten the palette.

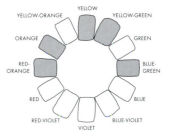

PALETTE #4

Analogous colors ranging from pale yellow-orange through minty green are elegant and understated. A neutral gray lends sophistication and pushes the scheme beyond "pastel." This palette shows how disparate hues become kindred colors when they are similar in value. Slight differences in intensity add an element of surprise.

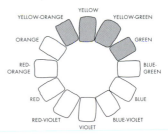

PALETTE #5

Primary red, blue, and yellow, known as a triad (page 17), work well when the colors are dark in value and low in intensity. In this palette, brick red, cadet blue, and palomino gold set a quiet mood. Green cools the warm red and gold; light khaki is appropriate for walls or trim.

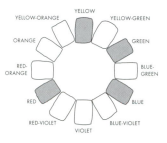

PALETTE #6

A limited palette of analogous colors looks complex when the values and intensities vary. The color range shown here is quite narrow, from warm ocher yellow through cooler greens. Dark gray and glen green anchor the scheme. The lighter values are appropriate for walls.

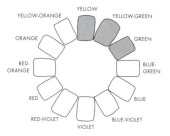

PALETTE #7

New neutrals (pages 14–15) in a mix of light, medium, and dark values make up a warm palette. Closely related values of toast and charcoal repeat the colors for a pleasing visual rhythm. Oatmeal and chamois are suited to walls or trim, browns and grays to furnishings and floor.

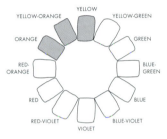

PALETTE #8

A six-color palette, loosely based on a near-triad (page 17) of yellow-green, red-orange, and violet, is diverse and complex. Aubergine and plum temper the warm olive green, gold, and russet. For walls, use either of the lightest values, or seek out lighter, low-intensity versions of the darker hues.

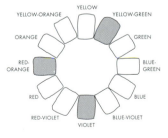

PALETTE #9

A light-value, clear violet adds an element of surprise to a classic blue and green combination. Pearly gray, a true neutral, spaces out the color, while a dark-value, low-intensity blue grounds the scheme. For a light look, consider gray walls or lighter versions of violet, green, or blue.

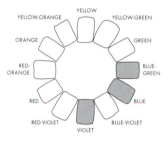

PALETTE #10

A palette of yellow, blue, and green is always fresh and summery. Varying the greens from yellow-green through green takes the scheme beyond the predictable. Slightly different blues—one true, the other closer to aqua—show that color combinations are often more interesting when you "wander around the color ring" a bit.

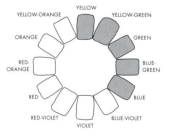

PALETTE #11

Warm and cool grays harmonize with icy blue-grays. Consider using the light gray on walls, the lightest gray on trim. A cool blue-and-gray palette benefits from the warmth of wood furniture or wood floors.

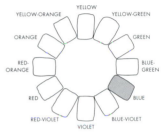

PALETTE #12

An analogous combination begs for a range of values and intensities, as in this yellow-green through blue-green scheme. A low-intensity yellow-green warms up the cooler hues. The light and medium values are suited to walls; the darkest green is a natural for furnishings.

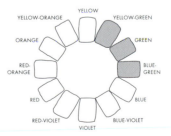

PALETTE #13

Intense, high-contrast colors are energetic and visually exciting. Two warm and two cool hues balance the visual temperature in this vibrant scheme. When you use intense colors, be sure to vary the quantities. Black and white, true neutrals, provide visual relief in a high-contrast room.

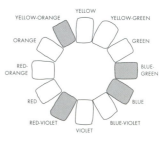

PALETTE #14

Analogous hues ranging from yellow-orange through red-orange couldn't be warmer. Varying the values and intensities just a little quiets the scheme and provides needed visual relief. Copper, a dark value of orange, tones down the brilliant colors. Use the lighter values for walls and trim, the darker values for furnishings.

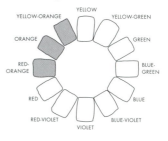

PALETTE #15

Near-complements of blue-green and red are tempered by a grayed yellow-green. Intense orange and yellow-orange push the scheme toward the warm side of the color ring. Consider lighter values of the warmer hues for walls, darker values of the cool colors for floors, and a mix of colors for furnishings.

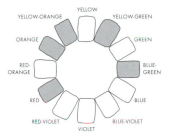

PALETTE #16

Complementary yellow-green and red-violet are stretched to include truer and bluer greens. A neutral the color of putty is appropriate for walls or floors, as are the light-value greens. Low-intensity red-violet is a natural for furnishings, with russet and green as accents.

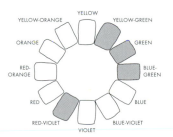

design credits

PHOTOGRAPHERS

index

Page numbers in **boldface** refer to photographs